A list of your author's books
are attached in the back of this
book for your inspection.

Staying Alive on Planet Earth 2

Psychology of Health Guidance
for determining which avenue
to take in obtaining better
health for longer life

Lloyd E. McIlveen

Order this book online at www.trafford.com
or email orders@trafford.com

Most Trafford titles are also available at major online book retailers.

Print information available on the last page.

ISBN: 978-1-4907-2906-0 (sc)
ISBN: 978-1-4907-2905-3 (e)

Trafford rev. 12/03/2015

 www.trafford.com

North America & international
toll-free: 1 888 232 4444 (USA & Canada)
fax: 812 355 4082

Introduction page

This extended version of Staying Alive On Planet Earth is offered and somewhat embellished for those of whom have acquired enough interest for aspiring to stretch their scope a bit more on longer life perception, approach and programming for that purpose.

Preface

The book on Staying Alive On Planet Earth#1 was a comprehensive and psychological view along with some health aspects and tips for those who were not sure what they wanted in the field of health and longevity. It was also a significant stepping stone for those who have decided to and are already practicing the art, if you will, of becoming and maintaining better health for longer life.

This segment of Staying Alive On Planet Earth#2 is a sequal to that coverage of health and survival. Those who have read and hopefully studied the book in a repeated manner are or may be prepared for an extended view because that is what staying alive is all about; extending and repeating.

When this segment was written, it was first designed to be a new and separate volume from Staying Alive On Planet Earth. As your author was writing, a reality struck where these scripts are not mainly focused on the constantly expanding areas of nutritional support and maintenance, but are offered primarily as a constant psychological view of how to prevent adverse situations from happening which hastens early death and will increase awareness of how to extend life. In that process, your author has discovered that perception, which is the psychological view, has its limits in the area of describing collective ideas, guildlines and insight for working longer life programs. Stretching beyond those limitations may be unnecessary, so this sequal will be an addition for needs to handle the enduring but rewarding task of extending life at this time on planet Earth.

There will be more in the next issue of our inherent passion for more life.

The following long life objectives are what we strive for in the beginning of our efforts to live a much longer and more rewarding life. We learn to make these established goals become vested and depended on from day to day and year to year. They do become stronger and more reliable when practiced committably for the cause of which this book and this cause is about.

The contents are primarily designed to work the mind to prepare for living much longer. Without the knowledge in preparing "for" these efforts, the goals intended for this venture into a newly understood future may only be a wildly imagined fantasy and never really be accomplished. Even this preface is a form of preparing for what's ahead and be adhered to in a serious manner.

Each chapter explains general guidelines for the reader to adapt in the process of making individual choices for the preparation stages of this venture into one's future.

As the general guidelines are displayed, one may get a spark of enthusiasm which helps greatly for making these decisions of future consciousness.

Good luck in acquiring your new skills of staying alive.

Contents

Chapter 1

What is living a longer life?

What does it mean to you? Is it a challenge to retain a title of living the longest to satisfy the ego? Maybe it's more time to acquire more possessions, love or position in life. How about a sheer sensation of fanaticism for feeling body senses and/or even sensuality. Among numerous other reasons, there may be a view in reality where life on Earth is all there is and one must grasp as much as possible because it will never happen again which can be an inextricable form of greed (endless need).

The desire for a longer than normal life means to one person that of which may be completely different to another. A "group" of people as compared to one or two, may have difficulty agreeing while certainly gaining more perspective on what reasons are best for this inspiring adventure into the future.

Living longer can be just that, an adventure into an inscrutable and unscrupulously known future ironically which only we humans create, but can also emanate challenging, exciting and unpredictable rewards.

However, it does mean more time on Earth, wherever it goes. One may have an affinity for peace and quite and never got enough of it. One of the priorities for that long life, which may be good health, will obviously be just one of the ongoing goals one must strive for while extending that life.

Certainly, one will not attain and sustain much of that longer life if attention isn't seriously paid to improving and maintaining the suggested, acquired and ongoing health.

Generally, when people are young, their survival aspects of life are focused more on gathering what is necessary to promote the immediate cause such as learning how to socialize, learning how to work and be creative or conform and/or experience intimacy for purposes of procreation or pleasure among other recreational activities.

Who thinks about longevity at that time even though they are being "hooked" on those acquirments and might, if they were ready, want them to last longer?

When they finally arrive at an earthly desire to extend it all, many times they discover through life's abuse, they have burned themselves out, so to speak and surrender any previous desire they may have had to live a really long life. Their ground down and exploited perception dictates it is too late! This type of thinking is a disease and can be conquered through realizing, which is an education, that disease can be reversed therefore allowing clearer reception and perception if discovered soon enough. Soon enough means before the disease becomes terminal: Most schools of reality state all plant and animal (including mankind) pass through a living metamorphose stage which is an irreversible expiration condition prior to final death. This is the only time when noncontagious disease cannot be reversed the same as when a plant turns brown where the roots are going through the natural process of expiring and nothing can stop it.

Other than that gloomy inevitability, noncontagious disease "can" be reversed with proper attention and TLC through wholistic, psychological and some medical application; sometimes more medical applications.

Knowledge with those said applications allows almost everyone the opportunity to choose a way for longer life. This becomes a belief system and it is by virtue of that belief system, where reality forms the truth of longevity existence. Efforts, as always, are required. Anything worth having are, most of the time, somewhat equal to efforts applied.

Long life is having more time to learn how to become healthier so one "can" live longer.

Long life is having a second chance for life on planet Earth.

Long life is having more time for making or saving more money or assets for the family etc.

Long life is for anyone who wants more time to broaden their minds. More power to them.

Long life means more time to find or discover what they may have thought they wanted earlier in life.

Long life allows plenty of new insight to flow with the times, life and special situations.

Long life allows one an extended ability to experience security within for the benifit of living "anywhere" in the world.

Long life can mean taking advantage of constant improvements in psycho and biological healthcare.

Long life can mean gaining knowledge sufficient to guide younger people in the prevention and control of what appears to be an inevitable population explosion. Presently, only happenstance controls malignant increases in population. Certainly there isn't much help from humanity.

Longer life means most people will be younger and need advice and/or guidance to understand their birth rights are meant to be utilized in making firm and uninfluenced decisions about life, health, belief and longevity while they are young and alive.

Children possess birthrights to choose as well as young people, adults and older folks. Life for living longer is usually appreciated more as one grows up or older.

Sure, life beyond the norm can occur by happenstance too. It just isn't inevitable with everyone and a little unreasonable to assume that kind of luck.

There are no standards or signs issuing longevity. Besides, happenstance isn't an accomplishment. Choosing to nourish a longer life with its challenges, whims, whams and uncertainties "is" an accomplishment.

Taking one's own life is not a viable solution when "inner" problems become insurmountable. Learning how to cope with those problems is. Insecurity resulting in death is the reverse of tackling those problems. Conquering those inner problems enforces drive for and allows longer life.

Living longer deserves, at least, the unwavering support of longer life philosophy and its movements.

Longer life is to be achieved by those who appreciate it.

Longer life is the ultimate of life's achievements.

Purposely surviving is an accomplishment of overcoming the anguish and sorrow of "losing" those who are close and loved which is a realization of that being as much a part of life as being born or dying.

Do not "knock," but underscore repitition where value is significant. Repetition in longer life programming and consciousness "is" a significant contribution toward adding to that longer life. It will be realized as progress of efforts unfold. Keep on reading and practicing!

Chapter 2

Staying on track in preventing self-deception

Realistically speaking, staying alive on Earth is only perceived in two manners. One is in the religious perception and one in the scientific perception. Of course, if one is bent on possessing no belief in anything at all as apparently animals and insects do, there would be just that; an animalistic view of existing only as an alive entity. No one knows what the animals are thinking, so a wild guess of them not even being conscious of long or short life to expedite a birthright for longevity may emanate the no belief at all consciousness limits of any possibility of there being a third perception in choices.

Usually, arriving at a point of staying focused on almost anything, one must visualize a larger picture than just a few minor details unless one just desire's minor results.

Extending life on Earth or anywhere else "is" and does require extending one's broader perception. Be ready to do that!

If one is instinctively and inherently reared or somehow endowed with abilities of perpetuating longevity, that person has and is developing a broader scope and is in a much better position to help guide others with similar desires and goals. Like any other endeavor, some will move forward more dynamically and/or easily and others will do what is basic or necessary. Following up will be those who barely drag their bottoms in efforts to grasp as much life as possible.

Regardless of their differences concerning ability, each one "will" broaden in their own way and be right as long as they remain constantly aware of their willingness to pursue and maintain a firm belief living a much longer life on Earth is the "right thing for them to do."

The religious view may influence some to deny any desire for a longer life where the earlier termination of life; the earlier one will reach heaven. All is fair to say and do in love, war and spirituality, so to speak.

Religious or scientific, they are both powerful! Either one can ingratiate an inspiration to broaden one's scope for living a longer life; on Earth that is.

The religious view in believing "can" extend beyond just like the years of life even though archaically established rules and guidlines may have restricted the use of self-realized and self-actuated beliefs concerning one's destiny.

By the same token in philosophizing, the scientific view of longevity is also belief oriented except more evidence is required for evaluating any project, contention or question.

Both the belief views, even though they may be different or even opposite, are mental energy poised for determining a choice for or not for longer life commitment.

Choice to commit for longer life is the key that opens the lock that prevents self-deception. Denying one's self an opportunity to make that choice is preventing a well deserved extension of life. It is locking that opportunity to add more and better life.

Self-denial because of inhibit oriented programming must be nurtured to expand its scope. Then, unlocking can be initiated by vocally expressing a statement to the self such as, "I want to broaden my perception so I may learn how to gain knowledge for longer life." That will be a beginning in the process of rejuvenating one's mind and body for the journey into living longer. Must we humans deny this opportunity because of being older or believing in "average" life span? Repeat the "I want to broaden my perception—daily."

No, we humans do not have to accept conventional "reality" of withering away at 70 or 90, especially when we program our minds, stay focused and look forward to expanding our perception and stay on this planet.

Self-deception is so easy to be trapped or locked into. Maintaining a purposely led conscious awareness of how the self thinks allows one to make mental adjustments for specific goals in particular pertaining to living a longer life. If one doesn't do this, that locked up and archaically oriented belief system of "I am right and you are wrong" will continue its catalytic nature of staying locked up and prevent the needed perception to expand; hence, justify "It's too late," or "What's the use?" or "I don't want to be old." How about the negative "Everyone else will be dead." The kingpin of them all is "Our maker determines the length of my life." No one knows that. It is acquired belief only.

If people choose to accept circumstances which shortens their lives with a helter-scelter and very risky mentality where "It is the will of our maker," that is truly their right choice for them. Also, if somewhere along the line of life, a man has a desire to expand beyond what has appearances of restricted views in spiritual perception and is unable to accept leading his own destiny, he is at the crossroads to decide his fate whether to tempt reality and go for more life or remain limited with conventional beliefs of deity controlled destiny. It's all in what we choose.

Your author preferes to think mankind can utilize their birthright intellect to offset and/or flex with time, circumstances and highly influenced beliefs to rise, develop and expand beyond many of the rules and deceptions of self and society oriented limitations.

Many of these linguistical additives can be advantages for staying on track in preventing self-deceptions which are stumbling blocks toward any intended goals.

Everything of any meaningful value begins and/ or ends with the self. Need proof? Take the self away and the values follow. Reminders untangle and clarify's goals.

Whether one is of a conventional believing nature and believes in deity destiny or whether one has acquired a philosophy of accepting responsibility for that destiny, longer life "can" be developed. It's only the approach to it via a belief system which will allow, disallow or initiate and promote it.

Whether it is a belief that "God" is directing it or whether it is a belief of "This is my choice," it will unfold in varying degrees depending on many factors such as birth conditions, beliefs, programming, praying and lifestyles. It will unfold, needless to say, with sincere and persistant efforts applied. Belief that longevity can be real is supported by effort.

Pro or con, good or bad, everything repeated becomes less intense; hence more enjoyable.

Staying on track with established guidelines and goals "does" prevent self-deception (contradictions, confusion in beliefs, lying etc.). It is also supported by continuously looking forward to longer life and its amenities.

Day to day or one day at a time existance is okay for short term purposes, but when one adopts a philosophy for longer life, one must become future minded. Our "track" is only as good as the way we build it.

Living longer, to some, is just a matter of "putting in their time" and no effort is exerted. Unfortunetely, those people won't even have a track, let alone follow it.

Developing a track to stay on usually starts with a desire. Almost everything worth doing is desire oriented somehow. Living longer seems worthwhile for whatever reasons may exist.

What good is life just existing? Reason for life is better. The "spice" of life is "conjuring up" ideas for creating goals. That's where developing a "track" of some nature, as part of a basis that helps motivate the desire to promote longer life, becomes a psychological road to safely and steadily follow. After that, there will be more reasons to follow and more goals to strive for. Theoretically and at that rate, life can last "many" decades beyond the norm. Stretch your imagination!

One will never know just how one's future will unfold. That's where the wonders of imagination can stimulate excitment for even speculating what will really unfold. What a waste living a life only thinking it will be over in a few years. That's been our programming and it has happened because of not building a planned and programmed life of extended future. That's the value of building a track for our future. Build it. It won't hurt at all.

Chapter 3

Follow the leader,
create for yourself, both or?

Leaders of the world have led us for many millenniums into and onto almost everything conceivable from religious serenity through wars of conquering with all the glory to paradoxical progresses in technology.

They stretched their precious intellectual growth and abilities almost beyond imagination, at least from the view points of earlier mankind. They practically led us like cattle into unimaginal endeavors of a very complex age in time on planet Earth.

Sure, we have always had choices, but have we always utilized those choices to the extent the leaders have? More than likely not. The masses tend to follow the upper echelons. Would they effectively lead us to choose a life that would extend into the distant future or even thereabout? Probably not. Why? Let's see.

History, ancient to now, has unveiled strong indications world leaders of many types were, would be and are primarily concerned about their jobs or position in their short term of leadership or life itself. Do you suppose they could take time to consider the possibility of everyone becoming wiser as a result of purposely living longer into the future? They would be better examples set for the younger to follow where with that wisdom, leaders would no longer pass the buck of debt into and onto oncoming generations and other likely scenarios? Not likely; at least not with the present state of politics and job securities and insecurities.

Sure, some nations have better credit to manipulate and promulgate cash from others than their own source, but now the world is beginning to see these debt methods for progress work! Don't think for a minute other nations won't follow. When and if that happens extensively, world chaos of another nature will prevail and why?

One man or woman leadership with a small party assisting it becomes a detriment to the cause of serene and healthy humanity. Politics are becoming a disease of which neurotically inclined partisan methods are practiced where the main menu of progress is to defeat the opposition regardless of principles. All this happens when leadership in pyramid form exists without enough insight for the distant future. What does this have to do with health? Part of good health is experiencing the feeling of security and contentment. If the upper echelon experiences indigestion, those who follow will too in more ways than intestinal disruption. The factor of politically influenced lifestyle affects goals of longevity.

When the distant future, regardless of near or far, is not seriously considered, everything calculable will hinge on the now of time only. That's politics and the business of making money which is now going rampant along with Earth's population explosion.

Most everyone follows the leaders or shall we say directors? It's like religion and science or positive and negative. How about good and bad and endless versions of opposites existing with the other. The universe is abundantly supplied with these clashing comparisons. They too could be classified as good, bad or other opposition where known leadership and control makes it so whatever they may be.

Whatever or whoever follows is generally pulled into the core of its delemmas. So, in the midst of these confusing activities (no one really has control of it all) where leadership reigns, the followers for the most part, are unable to compete with them or even reduce the potential of their momentum.

However, all is not gloom and doom. When one "get's in touch with one's feelings," usually one is able to make changes. The same can apply with the exploitation of masses. An individual can comfortably break away from the magnetism of societal clutches with all its pyramidical influences and power not necessarily by consulting family, friends or professionals, but by being internally creative and literally talking to the self. Anyone can create a program of asking questions, getting answers and making statements to follow. This is the best manner in which to be a follower. They won't go bonkers! They may be surprised with answers and also confident as time passes in creating longevity philosophy individually for making changes and decisions of which they can realistically promote and live with.

When that ability and confidence is achieved, they can grasp on to or apply new insight as to what a bigger picture is in viewing longevity perspectively, what it may amount to and understanding there is more to this life than previously realized. That's when they can become the leader of their own selves. That's when they can confidently choose to a commitment for living a longer life by accepting a firm and comfortable position of daily discipline required. That position is similar to the responsibility held by business, national and international leaders. They can belong to the individual. Just claim it!

The broader insight needed for promoting that addition of life is the acquired knowledge of maintaining daily awareness of being creative in efforts to gain better health and lifestyle for that extension of life.

Being creative means do not slip backward into the old programmed habits of "just" living with whatever happens by the day. It means seriously utilizing the knowledge gained from Staying Alive On Planet Earth #1 along with, as mentioned in the book, other guidelines on health for "added" perspective. Just remember to stay focused on being constantly creative with the promotion of good health along with being "the" leader of that endeavor. Leading the self for gaining more confidence and good health in body and mind is what perpetuates even more confidence in and for more of the same etc., etc.

Do not be only the leader of the self without consciously gaining more confidence in promoting better health and stability because one supports the other.

Gaining confidence and strength in any of life's endeavors becomes more of a challenge as we age and must be delt with firmly and objectively or the machine of the mind will break down and the body will follow.

A little insecurity won't hunt in supporting a desire for longer life as long as it is recognized as a creative support similar to that of the butterflies in the stomach experienced before a performance on the stage.

Life is a stage and we are the performers. Example: The sun rises and my first question is, "What shall I wear today? What will be my role for today?" We can choose our role in life or let someone else do it. Life is how we lead or how we are led.

Chapter 4

An evolution of survival

Is this business of living a longer life on Earth something new? Why now? Where will it go?

An immediate answer to those questions would be only a guess or a belief. Looking a little further, there is again the religious and the scientific viewpoints. There are indications stated in religious history where mankind was placed on Earth rather suddenly at a point in time and had to pay a price for living a life of insecurity and problems from not resisting a temptation. Those indications tend to support why there is so much suffering in the world from that point in time to today. People became recipients of habit.

That particular religious viewpoint isn't really any more than a sheer belief and nothing else because of the lack of evidence supporting it.

Since there is more evidence supporting the theory of mankind and animals etc. being of the same basic and earthly makeup, logic states they all evolved and grew through the space of time. That's the scientific view. There is value looking into that subject.

According to the scientific view, mankind has been on Earth at least hundreds of thousands of years since inception as compared to considerably less time than that of the religious theory of appearance.

If mankind suddenly appeared in recent millenniums, they couldn't have learned how to survive fast enough into the present time.

Logical appearance state mankind earned the ability of survival along with their counterparts animals and insects etc. That meant survival was truly earned the long and tideously hard way over untold and maybe even unbelievable periods of time. The possibility and probability exists mankind inherited the obviously possessed mentality to direct the destiny and length of their lives whether they knew it or not.

The concept of longevity certainly isn't anything new in the ancient historical sense as compared to the religious manner in which mankind was more recently placed on Earth.

There have been many stories, in the scientific, philosophical, societal and religious archives since the inception of humanity's recording system, of wise men (they hardly ever gave the women any credit) who lived long lives. Sure, it's nothing new. It is, of course, questionable how long long really was. Just because they had long beards didn't mean they were particularly much older than the present old age.

However, in those days of long ago, their opportunities to extend life weren't as plentiful as they are now. Why? Mankind is only capable of accomplishing their desired tasks and/or ambitions by skills acquired from the unfolding progress time has offered.

Those offers of time only occur when mankind is somehow pressured into expanding their intellect. There have been many times in mankind's history where intellectual expansion laid dormant for long periods of time mostly due to earthly or weather conditions that inhibited their movements from one place to another.

We exist, in present times, with the exact opposite of those slow days of progress. In those early times of mankind, they couldn't even reach the trees for the fruit let alone think about expanding their minds for living longer and more meaningfully. We've come a long way! That is, of course, the evolutionary theory.

This business of living a long life was probably not very primary in ancient times. Surviving the forces of preditor consumption was undoubtedly the prevalent factor in that survival period of time.

Recorded history presents fair indications long life was probably increasingly prevalent when man's desires began to appreciate and progress into the expanding era of forming communicable and societal accumilations. They wanted more of everything!

Mankind became aware of their insecurities, vulnerabilities and experienced the reality where they were such small specs in this existance of life and wanted to be bigger and more powerful.

They did it! Their ego was maturing. Think of where we would be today without a constantly expanding ago to drive us.

Mankind devised systems of compensating for their insecurities by building things; almost anything; especially the things that may have reduced their insecurities and enable them to reach out further for more.

Then, many thousands of years later, religion began and the people formed recognition and belief they could have a forever of their lives with a new kind of security by going to another dimension of existance called heaven.

From that inception of belief consciousness, even though they were beginning to acquire naturally dominant instincts to survive and extend that survival, many were profoundly influenced with the power of suggestion to believe they would ascend into this other glorious place of the future and set a new course in the evolution of belief which temporarily lessened the instinctual urge to live in a materialistic manner on Earth for a "predestined" period of time.

Only recent millenniums have revealed men have reacquired serious desires for longer life; more specifically, in recent centuries. How about years?

Why now? Obviously there are many indications almost everyone wants more of everything; much more than they did thousands of years ago. The difference between then and now, though, is where it is realistically and reasonably possible to "have" everything or at least a good portion of it; even longer life.

That last desire of longer life mentioned has been "cooking" in the minds of humans only (animals and insects, at least from what we have learned, haven't yet acquired the smarts to promote it) in these civilized communities on Earth and this is the right time for it to happen. We are poised to achieve significant strides of progress in living much longer lives. Let's take advantage of it while reducing overwhelming child birth.

The advent of higher states of consciousness and advancing technology has now allowed apportunities for living much longer.

Your author of this book not only writes and practices the psychology and application of better health along with the needed lifestyle for longer life, but also philosophically and sincerely supports the belief system that enhances longer life. Hopefully, that practice will be a contributing influence for those who have similar goals.

There are advantages for all when one practices survival techniques. When setting good examples, results will show and others will follow. It may be considered contagious again, as said, with the most needed reduction of excessive child birth for preventing chaotic overpopulation.

Chapter 5

What is really important with the meaning of survival?

Lining up our priorities is the beginning of what is really important for surviving in a longer term existance on planet Earth.

Generally, most of us think of our priorities as something we want or like to do and is great for experiencing desires and wishes. That tells us we are alive and want to exercise those dynamics in this life as long as we can. That's an average manner of dealing with surviving or shall we say living.

The "average" person, if you can accept that expression of the norm, is perpetuated through their life of survival more by emotional than objective desire. They want what they want and that becomes their drive to acquire. Those who live in less privileged invironments, passively or reluctantly, accept life as it unfolds usually without insight or desire to promote longer life. Surviving from day to day appears as the primary agenda. The meaning in affluent societies tends to be a desire for gaining and possessing more of everything including love, money, prestege, respect in relationships or position and many other accumilations.

The value and meaning of survival varies from lifestyle and status to religious and sheer invironmental conditions. They are rarely the same from one person to another.

However and wherever one may be geographically situated, the desire for longevity is not acquired by exposure to social degradation, genocide and dissease etc. or of the opposite being the intellectual clutter of possessions, greed and/or social position in life. It is acquired first by gaining clear understanding of what living longer than usual really intails to the individual in relationship with that person's environment.

The environment of humans, as compared to animals etc., is a definite and necessary factor in determining a self-promoted destiny of future orientation. How can we possibly have a desire for a much longer life on Earth if we have no knowledge, as examples, where we may only exist in a land of freezing snow, scorching desert, cruel imprisonment, daily earthquakes, comet raids or uncontrolled disease infestation etc.

Those are, indeed, extreme but possible scenarios and are suggested in the sense of realizing our choices (of course, if we believe we have them) of certain expenditures and sacrifices involved in obtaining that longevity will probably include some unplanned surprises in the trip of life's extended progress.

The negatives as well as the positives, if you will, must be scanned to determine if longevity is really what one wants. Clarity in desire is necessary.

Some people cling to and apparently enjoy avoiding the reality of what is and what may happen while in a state of fantasy. Longevity may cause an extremely confusing anxiety because long-term anxiety is not fun and can be intolerable.

Making the choice to live longer must be accredited to those who can and are willing to place that desire at the top on a list of priorities. Thinkers in fantasy only live for the moment and those moments are not filled with logical deduction. Choosing to live longer is logically accepting factors of change. Change is usually stressing and difficult to the point of preventing it thereby disallowing a strong enough desire for longevity let alone dealing with present situations.

Those who love to face reality and challenges of nature on planet Earth or even elsewhere, can line up their priorities in a clearly defined manner as to what longevity may have in store for them.

The possibility of religious views on longevity may influence making a decision to do it. Those views, in the conventional sense, contend God makes the decision concerning how long each individual will live. As long as one "hangs on" to the strict guidelines of conventional religion, accepting responsibility for extending normal life expectancy may be hindered thereby preventing the longer life desired. Because of that religious inhibition, the desire itself for longer life may be infringed upon. One must know one's self well.

There is much to be considered in making a decision for living a longer life. In some cases, it means dismissing the whole idea because of stringent and inflexible ideals and/or creed where the individual doesn't have the right or choice to make that decision. Sometimes the concept of longevity is only a fantasy of something not attainable.

Sometimes one lives a dynamically accelerated life committed to community affairs where slowing down for focusing on longevity would interfere with the agenda of progress and simply wouldn't fit in with a particular lifestyle and still others will decline because they believe they will be old, ill and/or withered out for too long in time. What they miss, in concept to living a longer life, is one must maintain a better fitness and awareness program and keep it going to the end which largely reduces the tendency to be "old and ill" thereby allowing longer life.

What "is" really important? After all is said, practiced or done, appearances seen primary, however it is experienced or desired, most people view life itself as "the" most important of anything when the bottom line is arrived at.

Chapter 6

Can staying alive be boring?

Staying alive longer may not be a matter of choice for some. Those who are not aware of opportunities to prolong life cannot appreciate that extended time nor do they strive for it.

Many nations of the world suffer unbelievable and unbearable hardships where domination of freedom exists. That domination includes depriving individuals of food and water, exposes them to genicide, extreme sexual abuse, identification robbery etc. and yes, many millions in bondage and forced labor slaves.

Those who have been conned, kidnapped and corralled to modern slavery (believe it or not, it still exists) who are fortunate enough to still be alive, exist only to stay alive let alone plan for a "long life." There are nations where some people only live to age 40 if they are lucky. Unfortunately, opportunities such as forced exploitation, doesn't allow freedom of choice.

Many of us are fortunate enough to be free, healthy and able to utilize our energies for our desires and have the wonderful privilege of choice in our lives. We can make decisions to promote staying young and trouble free. That's the beginning of extending our lives. That extension will be a direct result of preventing old age or, as it may, preventing the normal forces and influences that accelerates the aging processes.

There are those who instinctually believe doing nothing is a means to living a long life. One must realize doing nothing is just existing and could be termed as boring. Boring, on a constant basis can be interpreted as a state of deterioration and as you may remember from previous notes in your author's texts, deterioration is a preliminary condition for dying. Dying has not been a popularly known requesite for promoting long life!

Just existing and hoping long life will follow or just exist with no concern of staying young and trouble free will, in "most" cases, yield a net result of bearly making it to an old tired age from doing nothing. Of course, there are always some exceptions.

Many times and unfortunetely, animals apprehended from the wild have lived shorter lives in captivity because man has restricted their natural freedom to move, hunt, fight and be instinctually intimate.

Humans, being of the animal and insect species of living things will, on the average, shrivel up from inactivity as compared to growing into vivacious health. With luck, they may live a little longer than the average, but their lives will usually amount to a "milk toast scared to move," if you will, existance and many times end up as a commonly called vegetable from being withered.

It's great to appreciate just living for that experience, but isn't it meaningful or even a matter of being necessary when one can experience the exuberant resiliance and youthfulness of which good health offers even at 125 or so.

As repeatedly mentioned in these texts on longevity, being of the nature and having the desire to live longer isn't just existing. It's a matter of staying in shape with a purposely strived for youthful attitude that life is for living; which means growing in some manner or other to prevent said aspect of being bored and withered.

The "attitude" of "it's too late" or "at my age" or "you can't win" will most certainly deter any path to a longer life. How about when one says, "My family has a history of young death, so I don't have a chance" or, "My father died young, so I probably will too." Again, the word poppycock comes to mind.

Our individual span of life is largely a result of how we handle it and that's the truth!

Handling our lives is the main factor in the success of longevity. Some are lucky to be born into a family of emotional and nutritional support with purposely guided grounds contributing toward living a longer than normal life. Others, needless to say, may only learn what is available and/or the concept and/or choices of living longer at a later time in life. There again are those who have "developed" the defeatist view where time is running out and it's too late to do anything.

Being programmed to prepare at a young age, learning a chosen philosphy for longer life somewhere in the interim or finally discovering a desire (serious or not) for at least somewhat of a longer life later in life are all perceptions. Without those perceptions (many do not experience them), nothing will begin in the blessed art of purposely extending our span of life.

That striving for longer life won't be boring because it's like anything else that's worth doing. It takes effort put forth and effort put forth is being busy and being busy pursuing. It cannot possibly be boring especially when it is done with an open and even joyous attitude of creating something of which we can pass through to oncoming generations. The belief will make it so.

Sitting and waiting for the end of life just may engender it's inevitable course. Preventive methods, of which are many as noted in Staying Alive On Planet Earth #1 and other well knowns really work! They just need to be seriously and continuously applied and maybe even increased a little with the accumilated numbers of age.

Living and practicing preventive and stimulating methods for life is not only necessary, but also fun for longer life especially when enjoyed with the accompaniment of others who have similar views.

Extending life is challenging. How can that be boring? Being excessively tired may create an illusion of being burned out and useless. Just remember, though, unless it is a completely terminal illness with death at the doorstep, the feeling of being "worn out" is only a feeling. Feelings can be influenced by the use of psychology, TLC and supplements. Those are all available. Even a defeatist attitude of feeling "can" be altered for ongoing desires and challenges to maintain and promote a better and more meaningful life that can extend, extend and extend!

Being bored can appear similar to that of a flashing light signaling reason to change that state of mind. Listen and look or ignore and fade. It's all okay. Don't feel bad about it. That's life—or is it death? Who knows? One thing we are increasingly aware of in this space of time is we "can" exercise our birthright to choose our immediate or long-term destiny more than ever.

Time passes with more earthly opportunities unveiling more than ever and those choices are equally abundant. Reason with choices prevents limiting oneself to old time and conventional manners which create barriers to the progress of freedom in thought. There is no room for boredom anywhere anytime where there is an existance of freedom to do and be.

Chapter 7

Formula for acquiring and enjoying longer life

Sure there is a formula. You can devise one too. Just line up your factors for the formula in any position you choose. Be careful, though, the self can sway from the main focusing in choosing! Everyone is formulating one way or another. Just ask them. They will tell you what to do! Your author's formula is as follows:

Everything is not for everyone all the time as usual. It's like consuming vitamins. How much is really needed at the time since the body's needs vary with time? One solution, beside exhaustive medical testing or the wholistic method of kineseology (muscle testing), is to stagger the estimated amount daily arriving at a reasonable average which may, more than not, prevent over dosage at least. Under dosage is not usually considered hazardous and can be gradually increased with tests or feelings of well being, generally.

That vitamin analogy is only exemplary and somewhat limited in scope only to nutrition. The bigger picture is what is applied in activity toward gaining longer life in general which many of us have learned to appreciate in this time of desire for more of everything.

Factor h in the formula is equal to the constant promotion of better health from any age (the sooner, the better) and is high on the list of factors that can place one into a position for the goals of longevity.

Part of the h factor of "effectively" developing good and better health is how it is directed or guided. Assumptions without proper guidance must be left by the wayside. They are wild guesses and are insufficient for the cause of promoting the better health desired. Proper and effective support for that promotion requires following already established guidelines or "rules," if you will, from studying literature on health that has been proven by the test of time and growth in that area to increase better health specifically for the benifit of longer life; not particularly for aesthetical value.

The h factor includes being reasonably enthusiastic, not fanatically driven to the brink of burn out in the quest and passion for longer life.

Longevity is factor l in the list of factors for longer life and is the ultimate of all the preliminary and ongoing goals which is to determine what is desired before commencing.

Since we are formulating, health is referred to as a factor in the passion and quest of living much longer.

Aside from the technical rhetoric for a moment, health is usually considered the most important aspect of building and maintaining body stability for the long or longer run of life.

The promotion of better health for longer life many times is assumed to mean dealing with diet and exercise only. Sure, they are large contributing factors. However, be aware that diet and exercise can be readily interpreted in vastly different views. Examples are when one cuts down on hamburgers and consumes more vitamins and milk. It's okay, but what is that person replacing the hamburgers with and "is" the milk really as good as that person thinks it is? How about, "I gave up liquer and sweets. Now I eat pizza and diet soda." Others may overaccelerate lifting weights and drinking beer which is great for immediate effects, but is not condusive toward the preservation of organs such as the heart and others.

Factor ra is the rational approach to make good judgments when deciding to change course on the road to longer life. Time unveils requested wisdom.

Ask (whomever or whatever) and you shall receive. Just use it prudently.

One of the keys that unlocks the door of success in health for longer life is the discovery, approach and application of improving better conditions that can be maintained continuously. Stress, strain and overdeveloping "anything" is applying a detriment to longer life.

Many health procedures are devised and contentiously supported based only on what the individual conjures or believes and not necessarily from what has been studied or advised by accredited health care practitioners or long term methods proven from experiences and practices of people similar to your author who has gained that knowledge.

What instigates all this preparation for longer life? This is one of the most important in the factors for longer life. There must be an instigator or nothing of any real value will occur, especially on a constant basis. That instigator is the needed desire supported by the directing headquarters of the mind. That is the "psychology" that motivates the direction of moving forward. It's a commitment to do it! That's the factor ps in the formula which is the psychology of gaining constantly new insight and ideas for being uniquely creative with the realization that extending life is a result of extending the creative resources of the mind. What you put into it is, generally, what you get out of it.

Once again, without those orders and directions to move forward with commitment, nothing happens. Keeping aware with the desire to live longer must be paramount in the psyche. As such, it will secure the drive and ability to direct the show of effort in accomplishing that longer life.

One could say, "That's all too complicated!" There is a good chance it "will" be for those who "cling" to that possibility and attitude. By the same token, eliminating that defeat type stance by saying, "I can do it. I will do it. I am doing it" will reduce the self-inflicted barriers that cause resistance in "clinging" to negative attitudes of fear. You "can" do it! If in doubt, just practice saying, "I can" for awhile. It works.

Factor r deals with accepting responsibility for health application practices which includes more than just diet and exercise. It includes preventive methods in other areas. Health is also affected by social and environmental pressures and other inconvenient surprises. Maintaining defensive measures for safety and life preservation is wise and can be not only helpful, but possibly critical at times which means:

Stay away from hazardous environmental and social involvment that may lead to serious detrimental exposure such as wars, fires, floods, earthquakes, chemicals, accident potentialities, exploitation, kidnap, rape and genocidal possibilities, contagious disease and the list is long. Stay away from those who are obsessed with anger, envy, jealousy and even greed. Stay away from situations that may suddenly require having to compromise such as being robbed or abducted as mentioned. As populations expand, so do those potentialialities. Stay away from financial schemes and indebtnesses, unhygenic and unhealthful exposure and jobs or excitement that narrow the odds of staying healthy or even alive as planned.

There are many other trouble potentialities of which we need to offset related with health deterioration for the mentioned long life desire and/or maintenance.

Factor d is the discipline used as momentum of the strictly established reasoning to continue. Without that strict reasoning, the other factors may lag.

Factor e is exercise of which again is disturbingly viewed in different manners. Some people only walk believing that is the solution to the exercise question. Some workout on machines. Some only dance. Some think sex is all they need for exercise and others believe housework gets it. Would you believe playing cards? Most of the time people justify doing whatever is easy is good enough. That is usually not enough benificial design of exercise needed to support longer life growth. What they miss is one must arrive at some kind of formula (or guidance) for living longer devised of a professionally, if possible, instigated plan which, depending on the individual's circumstances, can be followed by a lifestyle suited to that individual on a constant basis.

Practice is pr factor. Practice makes perfect; like they say. It means repeating. One must understand what is involved with practice and the benefits or detriments from it. Practicing steadily bolsters that understanding (u in the formula).

Factor pe is perseverance. When one acquires and further develops a belief that longer life is desired, it's more than being constant in practicing the chosen methods and determinant inertia; it's being perseverant! When one realizes that perseverance is in motion, the confidence to continue is reassured and "allows" it to continue.

Factor di is diet which is frequently mentioned as one of the most important states of consciousness and application toward living longer. Follow the guidlines from "Staying Alive On Planet Earth" #1 and "reap the harvest" of health.

The total factors combined are the realization that longevity is an umbrella of extended efforts to secure health from as many angles of perception as possible and is supported by each stated factor.

Factors for longer life:

responsibility r	discipline d	rationale ra
understanding u	diet di	health h
practice pr	exercise e	longevity l
perseverance pe	safety s	psychology ps

Longevity unfolds after accepting responsibility of understanding, practicing and being perseverant with discipline in diet, exercise, safety, good judgment in exchange for better health and welfare that increases the extra length of life on planet Earth. Well, this formula may not be in algebraic form, but it "is" meaningful.

Part of the serious approach to better health is to refrain from excessive dependency on health care practitioners. They may not be constantly available for one reason or another. Willingly, you can learn to be more responsible for your well being by assuming more "interest" in your well being.

A well thought formula, regardless of its configuration, is meant to be helpful as a guide. If this chapter's formula seems reasonable and desirable, follow it closely. Otherwise, devise another way and stick with it or follow a well devised formula of some nature from someone knowledgeable who has a committed interest in this area of longer life sustenance.

Some people may find the use of formula type guidance too complicated or difficult to remember.

If that is the case, reread enough to get the general idea until the mind becomes more accustomed in its pursuance of better health. The steady addition of new health consciousness will add to retaining methods and manners of living with acquired health and of that way of life. Many people prosper by it. Others drop out and so much of the time and instances live shorter or less vibrant lives. Everyone has, though, the right to back off and pick it up later; much to their pleasing surprise. "I did it at one point in my life, but not for a very long period of time. I picked it up quickly again." L.E.M.

Chapter 8

Methods of staying alive

There are endless "methods" of perpetuating a cause of some kind in our lives such as maintaining a religious or political continuity, business or trade extention courses or how to cure the drinking or overeating problems etc; why not methods to stay alive?

Let's get to the brass tacks of it all! Staying alive longer doesn't necessarily happen when one believes it's in a state of fantasy or because relatives lived longer. How about, "My psychic said I would" or "Oh, I don't smoke or drink."

The stability and continuity of living longer is very similar to a relationship, marriage, job, flying in an airplane or even to stretch the point a little, walking a tightrope. There are no guarantees; only risks and possibilities.

People fantasize and wait, sometimes a lifetime, for enough confidence or assurance to proceed with desires of fulfillment. They look for, not only assurance, but an actual guarantee; even though they do experience "some" reality where guarantees do not exist. Those tendencies to want control over the unknown are subconsciously frustrating to human progress which, of course, is limited to only a few years of life. Let's get with it!

The risks are only a "sign in the road" which says to be careful, use your head and plan. It also says we are now what we previously planned or didn't plan.

So, how do we stay alive? We do it first, by being fortunate enough to experience a realization where an extention of life or maybe even more, is possible and probable if we care and arrive at a decision to do it. Then it is manifested by a belief system in consciousness that becomes a way of life. There will be no going back to ordinary "falling victim to circumstances" mentality. When that lifestyle is realized, adapted to and initiated into "real" health and preservation activity, the ongoing maintenance and practices of proper and disciplined diet, exercise, attitude and responsibility for safety will unveil in its entirety according to planned efforts applied at the risk of repeating and that is what is needed too. "I do it too." L.E.M.

All food must be fresh, clean and eaten on a regular basis. Remember, best results are acquired when established guides are practiced. That means outside opinions on longevity lifestyle must be respectfully ignored. Unless they can follow good examples of longevity practices, they will probably be opposition hecklers and may create resistance to the cause. They too have their rights of opinion and lifestyle. Just let them keep it to themselves. They may only want money.

The first book, if you didn't read it first on "Staying Alive On Planet Earth #1" has a comprehensive coverage on specifics of food, general nutrition and digestion. Staying Alive #2 is written as a "boost" for acquired psychological perception gained while practicing better health for longer life as a result of reading and practicing from the first book.

Moving along, exercise can be interpreted as equally important for staying alive longer simply because, to begin with, the food is less effective as energy fuel in the arteries and veins if they become clogged. Sure, you may be eating better food since you have joined the clan of the plan, so to speak, but the existing, density and flow of blood through those arteries and veins have jeopardized the quality and action of those fully invested efforts of administrating more nourishing food by allowing them to stagnate and clog. The main necessity and function of exercise is to maintain blood clarity by accelerating the flow of blood so as to "wash" the inside walls where plaque clings and builds up from the accumilation of cholesterol, calcium, tar, fat and other clogging influences as specific enzymatic substances. Description of specific heart disease is displayed by your author in the first book of Staying Alive which has the same subtitle of Psychology of health guidance for longer life.

The second necessity and function of exercise is for maintaining and yes, keeping muscle tone and joint stability. This, along with pure blood flow, allows one to continue the program of long life progress.

Third, but not necessarily last is exercising for "all" body systems which include psychological balances that allows feeling vibrantly alive, not just existing. Further, as your author refers to occasionally pertaining to issues of health, love and relationships, "perpetuate" the desire to continue with the plan. That is one of the many available keys that can unlock the doors to being successful with attaining longer life; perpetuation. It's been said perpetual motion is impossible. That may be true when it pertains to mechanical apparatus, but not with consciousnesses of the mind!

There are many attributes of which can inspire one to excel in health, but may not necessarily enhance excitement enough to further the cause such as the purely exilerating enjoyment and the exercise aftermath of relaxation. Many longer life attributes, in the balance of those mentioned, will be consciously noticed when one continues with the program.

So far, we have covered some of the importance and significance of diet and exercise consciousness with the realization of that being only a good sized part of the program.

One of the last principle basics to consider practicing, while gaining all this good health, is preventing any or further disease or accidents which may trigger or add "to" disease or related illness.

Do not be paranoid, but maintain awareness that close exposure to other people or even animals and insects may create life threatening conditions. Be careful and do not use drugs, alcohol or smoke. If you are not careful in those preventive measures, odds are you will not reach those later years. Being careful also means to extend efforts in preventing accidents whatever and wherever. They are a huge cause in the "prevention" methods for longer life.

Other areas necessary for attaining and retaining for longer life are somewhat repeats again and won't be mentioned at this time. That is what is involved in this business of staying alive, staying focused on a plan or program and repeating the steps learned for that accomplishment.

The notes in these texts are fairly general and can vary or be customized for the individual. Developing a firm belief in your program for staying alive for a longer period of time will suffice with pleasant rewards.

One of the most important methods attributing toward living a longer life is maintaining an awareness of what is really important. That means what is "seriously" important and cannot be taken for granted. It's about the heart. Life can remain in existence without food and water or necessary life supporting substances on a temporary basis and maybe even longer. However, life of any living beings or plant life is perpetuated by the element of growth primarily, not food, water or air. Life begins with a movement. That movement is the beginning of growth. That growth immediately starts life in plant and animal (all life on Earth) and very suddenly ends life. The only difference between plant and animal is the pulsating organ; yes, the heart; the movement of the heart. The heart is a muscle and we must remember to treat it as such.

Sometimes living beings and plant life appear to be dieing, but are technically not until the fuel for growth stops flowing. So, it is not the heart or the fuel for growth that initiates dieing. It is the ceasing to grow that dictates it. Nothing stays alive, like starving roots in the ground, that doesn't grow somehow. Illness or aging is an example of a preliminary shrinking process.

Living a longer life has the same signifacance. Remembering and practicing requesites for growth will extend life. The heart is "the" most important attribute to be considered in evaluating the course of human care and cure. Extending life will not happen in an approximate manner. That's pure fantasy. It will either continue with purposely led growth or it will shrink or plug-up for lack of integrity. Growth is what leads the way toward extended lifespan. Think about it. Getting best results for longer life requires one to know the heart is a muscle and must be delt with and cared for as such. Exercise, proper nutrition, less stress and chemical exposure along with sufficient rest allows continues growth.

Most of us are highly influenced by our families, friends, employment and business associates, a lover and even whether to go, be or live in certain areas or environments detrimental to our longevity cause. If that is true, life can be a detrimental vacuum pulling us around from pillar to post in the process of social magnetism. Life can also be restricted by that magnetism. Whatever the case, the lifestyle adapted in those areas is more influence than choice oriented and may not allow a "burning," if you will, self-focused desire of health behind that route of lifestyle. It's almost as though the individual is constantly led by others, as mentioned in other paragraphs, instead of leading the self toward better health.

The individual who wants longer life has to "direct" the self in the lifestyle chosen by the self. Influence by others is the norm of the times and must be delt with in a reasonable manner to maintain family etc. (family can have a variance of meaning).

If a lifestyle from those influences drains one from longevity objectives, then it's time to make adjustments for staying alive.

The last and maybe even more important message for staying alive in this chapter is one of preventive methods. This involves the social technicalities of preventing HIV-AIDS.

There are misconceptions of how one may get infected with the aids virus. Kissing or being exposed to another person's seliva hasn't been widely accepted as causing the disease. The following will help to understand.

The aids virus is only incepted into the human system through the vulnerable paths of that system. The blood system is an open door for HIV to enter, stay alive and grow. That, as we know, is accomplished either with #1. an injection of an HIV contaminated medical syringe, #2. through exposure to a freshly open laceration or wound where the virus may enter or be forced into the blood stream or #3.

where the virus may enter the anus or vagina from penis sores or semen and passes through the colon or female organs which is a incubator for the virus while entering the bloodstream to dominate the system.

The assumed, surmised or contended posture where HIV is acquired through oral sex is reasonably defeated when one becomes aware the virus is alive moving from the mouth through the throat and into the stomach, but dies from the counteracting stomach acid therefore never entering the bloodstream. That has been the socially accepted theory unless one's system does't manufacture that acid.

Freshly bought male contraceptives do quite well in preventing aids exposure along with learning more how that virus functions. Respect for its potential is priceless in its prevention for one to remain healthy and live long.

Chapter 9

Reaffirming our efforts in reversing disease

Disease is a huge factor in the formula for living a short or not very long life. There truly are applicable methods available especially for preventing disease as well as curtailing or submitting them to a remission state.

Some diseases begin at birth; an inherited disease which, unfortunately, is usually virus oriented and not preventable unless efforts are applied to curtail the debilitating or spreading affects. Longer life to them can only be perceived as striving for as much short life as possible. Some living beings have lesser potentialities than others and have to strive more diligently because of very low immunity to specific virus.

Other inherited diseases such as Alzheimers has potential for evolving in family members, but the odds are limited, fortunately, to a smaller percentage of that family acquiring it. So far, Alzheimers can only be patiently delt with, but not easily prevented. The same applies with multiple sclorosis and a few others that are, unfortunately, not favorably preventable.

Contagious disease, as venereal and hepatitis, are only prevented by nonexposure or contraceptives etc. They are treatable, but not completely extinguishable. They are not popularly known, when untreated, to help in the process of achieving longevity. However, modern science has applied successful efforts in eradicating the effects and the outlook for longevity is more favorable than not with these diseases.

HIV (aids) is another story. It is definitely a life shortening disease either when ignored or realized too late. The only preventive protection one has is to refrain from sexual exposure or be real strict with contraceptives. The alternative to that is risk and susceptibility to contamination; hence, easy to get! Aids is treatable better now than ever, but living with it and the drugs are not an attractive manner in which to optimistically pursue living an extended life beyond the average unless super determined. That's reality! The other side of the coin has it there are always possibilities of improvement with the passage of time. Wonders in science and belief never cease.

The good and better news is disease prevention and remission efforts do work and quite effectively in most cases where objectivity, sincerity, persistence, belief, openness, the formula and its amenities, plus practice are concerned and applied.

The guidelines in the first book of Staying Alive On Planet Earth on nutritional criteria are a great source in disease prevention.

Disease prevention can certainly be interpreted as more important than the treatment of disease. If people would prevent them, they wouldn't have to treat them.

Prevention of disease usually means prevention of self-inflicted disease; not necessarily disease acquired from exterior influences. Most self-inflicted disease is "built" within the self by inferior nutritional consumption, poor health hygiene, smoking, drinking alcohol, using drugs and a disseminating array of other personal and interpersonal influences, activities and other intakes. It pays to exptrapolate on this.

Most nonthreatening diseases are self-inflicted through lifestyle conditions and are only tolerated, not effectively treated. Note: That unattended toleration can reduce a possible extention of life!

Needless to say, attempting to brief on all the self-inflicted diseases would be a time consuming task, so a few descriptions of general and preventable illnesses of that nature will be listed plus common sense prognosis for the benifit of anyone caring to apply their efforts of prevention for possibilities in extending their lives:

#1. The common cold and allergies which are, much of the time, thought of as being the same. Some of the symptoms can be virus influenced and some can be instigated psychologically by drafts, weather and even strong beliefs of specific allergies. However they are acquired, being as still as possible and encouraging nasal drainage can assist the natural course necessarry. Over the counter remidies tend to cover up the symptoms and sometimes extends the duration of the cold, generally.

#2. Headaches, beside colds, are many time experienced from stress, hypocondria, improper food or liquid consumption, specific odors and exposures, excessive worry or combinations of them all. Other physical, mental or emotional defects may cause headaches which require professional examinations and attention. However, common headaches can be reduced by the use of common sense as examining reality a little more seriously, clearing out excessive toxins in the body with temporary fasting, enemas, colon cleansers, daily exercise and largely replacing bad habit food with simple and proper combinations. Check with the first book on Staying Alive On Planet Earth#1 for more specifics on diet etc.

#3. General nausea or sudden ill feeling from no apparent reason which causes vertigo (dizziness), vomiting and general weakness can be triggered by overeating acid making food when not consuming enough water to offset the acid. Check acid/alkaline list in "Staying Alive On Planet Earth#1. Apply that information with prescription or nonprescription acid reducers and the problem "can" be relieved along with reducing too much protein food. Professional help is wise.

#4. Cancer "can" be considered self-inflicted if one will accept the responsibility for their ills. It can, many times if not more, begin and be provoked by exposure to toxins which can evolve from an endless array of possibilities including being born with the blood of a contaminated parent, being raised in a contaminated area (industry of chemicals, radon on premises, filth etc.), being raised on junk type food and/or doing the same when older just to mention a few. These exposures deserve serious consideration, studying and change for reducing cancer possibilities.

External or internal toxin effects on the body's cells, which can be termed the responsibility of the individual, are innocent bystanders until they have carcinogenically mutated into cancer cells. Possibilities in preventing that condition exist. Examples: Do not fry or bake cooking oil. Do not breath or inhale unnatural substances as smoke or chemicals steadily. Do not consume manufactured food additives steadily. Cancer mutation transforms inside the body; even the skin type.

Once cancer begins to grew, just as most everything else in nature, it is similar to plant roots in that it will continue to grow as long as there is something to latch onto or grow for. Sometimes it is stated as "feeding" on. When ignored, it spreads mercilessly, sometimes slowly and other times quite speedily.

Even though the mass of the cancerous effect may have dimensionally increased and will not subside easily, the chances for initiating a condition of remission through natural methods are favorable in weeks or months and not as favorable in years when ignored, but can be slowly curtailed. Remission means reduce the spread of the growth, not necessarily to eliminate the acquired growth.

Following serious wholistic methods as outlined in the first book on Staying Alive On Planet Earth and my book, "Understanding Preventing And Eliminating Cancer" reveals acceptable to favorable results of natural methods for dealing with cancer.

The alternatives are drugs and surgery etc. which "may" cause minor to traumatic shock to the human system. The question of which is better is a subject of ongoing personal and professional belief and debate. The medical aspect of health and cure will not be expounded on in these texts except to say both wholistic and medical methods have their benefits and unfavorabilities.

#5. Heart disease appears in different forms. Most people only identify the disease as that of clogged arteries and viens and is usually the most widely spread of that organ's disease. Clogged arteries and viens are "the" most hazardous self-inflicted threat to life beside acquiring the "wrong person" for a mate. Sure, a stroke can play havoc too, but it may only cause debilitating or paralytic effects; not necessarily death. When blood in the arteries and viens cease to move because of plaque inhibition and no detour, life may only last a few minutes if not less when not quickly attended to.

Plaque can be prevented by refraining from the lengthy or constant consumption of specific processed food as mentioned in the first book, smoking (tar) and increasing a program of mild to exertive exercise preferably by professional guidance if feeble, elderly or handicapped along with practicing better health methods.

Chelation therapy has been known to be successful in reducing plaque. It is a somewhat natural substance administered by intravenous or pill form through wholistic practitioners (mostly chiropractors and some medical doctors who practice wholistic methods too).

The plaque type heart disease "is" self-inflicted by virtue of the self doing the consuming.

#6. Diseases related to digestion and the stomach are among a multitude of common ailments. The quality of physical and yes, emotional stability begins and journeys into a direction and existence of well being or deterioration. Well being is either basic luck of inheriting disease resisting genes or results of one being constantly digestion conscious. That means to arrive at a plan of some kind for maintaining proper digestion as eating pure food especially in a peaceful environment. The wrong food etc. accompanied by a stressful environment creates an imbalance and complex digestion function of its juices sometimes referred to as gastrointestinal disorders emanating from chemical reactions. The results are complaints of ongoing and nonthreatening annoyances one can attach a name to and support the growth of by blaming something or someone else instead of seeking out a solution to offset the problem.

Digestion illness can be prevented and rewardingly resolved to remission by accepting responsibility for initiating them regardless of relative, friend or institutionally influenced or directed. That possibility has real and adaptable value!

#7. Breathing, liver, kidney problems along with aches and pains of arthritus, fibromyalgia, constipation and other common ailments can be brought under control in varying degrees by practicing disciplined programs similar to what has been mentioned in these texts and in the first book. Extreme or emergency cases may require medical attention. Discretion in deciding must be carefully adjudicated because that too, is a factor in the success or not of accepting responsibility. Most of all these ills, problems and decisions fall into the category of self-inflicted occurances and will unfold as we ignor them or as we treat them. Reversing disease is an ever increasing trend at present and is destined to follow into the future with our acquired health awareness and procedures.

Remember, none of the self-inflictive diseases are exactly the same in all individuals. That's what makes diagnosis and treatment difficult. Realistically, it's all a guess. That is why being responsible for our existence is important. The more responsibility we accept, the better our chances are in supporting one another arriving at diagnosis and solutions for managing and curtailing illness.

Chapter 10

Do politics help with organizationally influenced health?

Do communities and governments drive the people or do people drive the communities and government? That is the question here and now. So what? What difference does it make in health for longer life? That also deserves probing.

None of those questions matter if you have no interest in getting help for living longer.

Most humans just forge along in life busy doing a lot or little while either avoiding or ignoring two vital points of life; health and length of life. They may be young, preoccupied with life's sprouting and have a "who cares" attitude or they may be older with families and careers etc. and unpretensious of their health for length of life let alone for the present.

Still, many retirees undergo more treatments than ever and also expect to be taken care of. Also, they begin to appreciate and want more life.

Doesn't anyone ever think ahead? Sure they do; just not seriously enough until it's almost too late.

Communities and governments are beginning the struggle to deal more effectively with health and sometimes there is a trickle of interest in longevity.

Organized communities (townspeople, investors, sector representatives etc.) hesitate on the "gut level" desires because the "gut level" of desires, in this case of health for longevity, is hardly ever announced or discussed. It's usually a matter of personal undertaking. Politically speaking, most people (residents and representatives) seem primarily interested in what they can materially or legally acquire for the supposed short term of either life or community office.

The multimega institutions who assume support and sponsorship of health assistance are either limited in scope of truly wonderful methods of preventing and render diseases hopeless to grow or only care philosophically and monetarily about resolutions for the present time with the attitude where the people will only live so long anyway.

The options and opportunities to gain better health for longer life is wide open and abundantly rich with ways and means to gain, maintain and retain those advances in consciousness and technology for longer life.

The politics of it all, at least at present, prevents the pure, lasting and meaningful aspects, affects and effects to materialize and become an inspiring segment of the health industry for those who aspire to live longer.

This will change for the benefit of health and longevity when the mass of people on both sides of the social agenda realize living for now is not really the most important of all. The health of future thinking concerning how to handle health in a no contaminating and natural manner will lead the way toward better health and longer life.

As the people and leaders of the future share and assimilate their changing values with the changing times from strict monetary values concerning health objectives, wholistic methods are becoming increasingly effective, popular and a permanent fixture in our health systems of the world and will be compatible counterparts with what is now considered a competitive industry.

When the societies of the country and the world finally decide to eliminate their competitive stances against one another, they will join with both their long acquired disagreements and expertise to form health programs for the benifit of, primarily, living longer. How they will do it remains to be seen. We are not quite ready yet. Be patient. It will happen.

The politics in the meantime are showing we must accept more responsibility, day by day, in practicing natural and preventive methods for offsetting toxin influenced methods to "prove" natural methods work as well if not better than conventional methods.

Again, natural methods in an extended version, are the consideration, approach and application of consciously acquiring a psychological perception of what one wants, what one is willing to study and practice and what one will be willing to continue with. All three are necessary.

Politics are an expediant plan and approach. Since politics are not particularly helpful in setting a pace with solving health problems at present, we must again, set our own political agendas as individuals by practicing combined efforts of natural and some scientific methods until the official politics deem it is time to follow us as good examples of longevity philosophy and approach for better health. Our healthcare industry of medical and wholistic professionals etc. are overdue to combine these two mighty methods of healthcare maintenance and cure. Let's help by taking more interest in learning more about these industries and what they "really" do.

Unfortunately, there have been many unsaid ideas, concepts, philosophies and downright secrets (for a better word) held back from the public concerning what can or would serve the public's best interests and needs in the industry, if you will, of "really" better health in sustaining and retaining that stance for a much longer existance on this planet.

The necessity and greed for money has been the primary impetus holding back the knowledge and creativity for producing mankind's dream/utopia type health scene for everyone. The intrepreneurial, business conglomerational combination controlling political aspects of health changes are usually at the core of where it all goes. Only time will change all that for now. The only solution there, again, is to do the best we can in living longer for realizing that wonder of what mankind "is really" capable of doing.

Chapter 11

Learning to flow along with surviving tactics

Living longer is not completely about diet and exercise. Oh no, we won't ascend into extended life on Earth that easily. Extra life may be considered a pure luxury when it is something we want more than anything else. After all, how can we have anything in that extra time unless we have the extra time? Anything we want, which is considered more, better or enjoyable, can be valued as a luxury.

Luxuries always have a higher cost. Sure, money can very well help in paying expenses for extra time. The costs needed more than money are those efforts which are constantly accentuated as a reminder to not take them lightly. It must become a profound part of the program for longer life. Rich or not, the price of efforts extended in daily practice exceeds the power of monetary influence.

Even though the wealthier have more money to invest in doctors, supplements, medicine, assistance, education, equipment, flexibilty in choices of where to live and other expense options, their tendencies are to live more of a plush lifestyle which means eating and drinking that which is palatable, not necessarily nourishing. They may like the idea of living longer, but when it comes to waiving their lifestyle of pleasure in exchange for the disciplinary form of life required for longer life, the bottom line reality may reveal a supposed high quality, faster and high type life is more important. Consequently, any previously considered desire for longer life may be indirectly relinguished because of overwhelming tendencies and habits. This is, of course, only a conjecture.

Considering the less affluent and poor, efforts extended for longer life have relative opportunities for extending life. Even though indications for longer life may appear somewhat monetarily oriented, the less affluent can assert more effort in gaining and practicing the many times mentioned better health and survival awareness in lieu of financial support for it.

What are the "tactics" needed to secure longer life? All that has been mentioned, so far, plus constant reminding by the self, by others or by reading these texts on longevity as many times as necessary to allow survival consciousness does encompass a great deal of detail to become an ongoing program of motivation toward this cause. Without the required and truly needed program of guidance, the actual day to day changes and additions may not adhere as well as expected. Constant reminding of the efforts mentioned must be persevered. That is worthy to the cause. Added preventive measures for longer life as reminders are:

#1. Use more fibrous food and less or no sugar for preventing constipation and related ailments.

#2. Drink more pure water for better circulation and cleansing. Distilled water is best, but one must consume mineral supplements as distilled water has none.

#3. Slow down! Tycoon and fast life style burns one out.

#4. Always keep the mind stimulated to prevent "old minds."

#5. Exercise is a necessary art. Remember, the heart is a muscle and must be constantly developed as any other muscle similar to #4, but not overexerted.

#6. Do not make enemies. They may cut your life short.

#7. Drugs, smoke and liquor kills. It "shortens" life.

#8. Never get into a position of having to compromise such as a domestic dispute where one is either emotionally or objectively derailed. The results may lead anywhere from ill health to a short life. Another general example is where one venture's into vulnerable positions or areas of robbery, rape, kidnapping or even genicidal exposure.

#9. Young people are generally accepted as healthier in the physical sense along with an assumption living long life will follow. That possibility may be erroneous and contrary to reality. Why? Let's see: If one reaches a middle age of around forty, that person has begun to appreciate a value of life itself and has also begun to reduce physical risks for preservation purposes. Younger people, especially men, involve themselves in activities of excitement, not preservation and are more susceptible to serious accidents that prevent ongoing life. The opportunities for younger people to live longer are greater because of what can be learned and practiced, but the odds are not favorable for that destiny. If they are lucky enough or have meaningful guidance in reaching the appreciative point of maturity, the odds will favor longer life. Perspectively and realistically, older people will assert themselves with prevention methods for longer life. Attention younger people: Become and stay aware of how the odds fit in with desires. Be aware of your own self-causing problems which may prevent longer life. Your opportunity to either increase or decrease the odds of longer life are at your disposal. Deceptive perception is the responsibility of the self. Once it is in conceivable motion, it is sometimes uneasy to change its route. Program your mind for your most profound, reasonable and "gut level" desires especially when there is an inclination to live into the reward laden existence of at least some of the future. Living longer is a great concept and could be a great accomplishment. Just don't deny yourself of extra time on Earth by allowing yourself to be precariously, confusingly and deceivingly mislead into illusions of living, somehow, forever. The possibilities are the same as any other possibilities. There just isn't enough evidence to support a need to live in some other dimension of space forever. End of preventive list.

The disposition and destiny of our human existance is equal to that of what we had at birth, what program we were raised with and what manner of beliefs we kept or chose after that. Our destiny for life's span is either to continue with our past rearing or choose another direction toward the balance of that span. We can also fall into an institutionally complaisant state of mental and emotional security as so many millions have in the past thousands of years; all of which adds or subtracts length of life on planet Earth. It's all a matter of belief. One states we are led and one states we lead. Generally, those who are led do not believe they have any choice pertaining to their length of life. Anyone who leads; exercises a birthright of choice and creates extra time with the knowledge of more time being an accomplishment for more time.

Anyone can add to the list of preventive measures for longer life. Just remember, the longest list in the world is worthless as a wooden nickel if not believed and practiced.

Younger or older, well or sick, rich or poor, smart and successful or not, every living person has that in common and we can all say, "I want more" and get it. It's there. Believe it.

Surviving longer is a challenge and a reason to be proud of that success.

> Living a longer life on Earth is a total result of general health, security and welfare consciousness motivated by the individual mind.
>
> Let's keep that "in mind."
>
> More improvement issues on living long will follow as they become published. This published issue is 2014. L.E.M.

Index

Your author, Lloyd E. McIlveen unveils a chronological list of many and various book subjects presenting controversial, educational, uplifting, futuristic, self-helping, philosophical, psychological, entertaining and other stimulating concepts of which are and will be displayed with brief descriptions of each book as follows:

1. "Evaluating Outdated Beliefs" This is a report, viewed through the perception of your author of the evolutionary process and changes occurring in belief; especially in the area of religion and spirituality. This was designed for the benefit of broadening individual perception, perspective and viewing "another" plane of belief while revealing fallacies in theological indoctrination. This is an improved revision of the book's origin.

2. "Staying Alive On Planet Earth I" This is a psychology of health required to stabilize and

maintain better health for the benefit of living a much longer life. Source: A lifetime of study, problems, recoveries and many successes more in natural methods.

3. "Understanding Loss To Relieve The Anguish" Loss of anything involves many distractions and disrupting emotional disarray. Gaining greater understanding of these emotions offsets the misery of them and enhances optimism of confidence and support for emotional weakness before, at and during the time of loss.

4. "Understanding Preventing And Eliminating Cancer" presents new views on the wonders of natural methods for practical use.

5. "Paradox Of Progress Unfolding I" This is a tale told by a man "many" centuries into the future about an exciting, overwhelming and terrifying occurrence on planet Earth as a result of their wondrous progress around the

time of 2300 A.D. Hang onto your seats! #2 is a second issue later on the list.

6. "Offsetting Climate Change And Nuclear Waste Contamination" This view of the two exposes the hazards, inevitabilities and possible solutions needed now for preventing a "too late" disaster that will affect all living beings too soon.

7. "What God Is And Is Not" This is a study of spiritual possibilities designed, not particularly to remold conventional mannerisms of belief, but to open and expand perception in the most controversial subject of mankind; the subject of God and whether mankind will or won't expand that consciousness along with all progress and growth on Earth and in the universe.

8. "Kids Of The Crick" This is a story of four old fashioned country kids setting out on a weekend adventure in their countryside of tall

grass, mountains, rivers, animals, caves and strange living beings. Sometimes, they aren't sure whether it's all real or not.

9. "Paradox Of Destiny Explained" eliminates the mysteries, facades, fantasies and deceptions of how, where, way and when we do what we do and opens new possibilities for expanding our beliefs and consciousness pertaining to this study of available options that may influence insight for growth, change or even justify present mannerisms of what may control the individual, planet Earth or the whole universe and is not zealous, fanatic or bigoted; only assertively revealing.

10. "Paradox Of Progress Unfolding 2" This book is a continued fiction story and can be considered exemplary of "major" human changes that alienated millions of people to another planet in the future. They are led by the elements of unexpected surprises of which

is par for the course with gutsy space pioneers. The first "Paradox Of Progress Unfolding I" must be read first to understand and appreciate the disproportional attitudes and positions of people on a threshold of major change and disasters upon them. This is not only a tale of travel, trials and tribulations, it is philosophically stimulating and adds toward future insightful expansion of the human species.

11. "Staying Alive On Planet Earth 2" This is all extended version of the original psychology of health for living a longer life. More knowledge allows more life.

12. "Preventing The Doom Of Mankind" This is a stimulating, vitalizing and somewhat shocking description of how mankind is "truly" faced with extinction in the "near" future due to their own faults of progress. It's very educational and needed now to help offset that inevitability

where the odds dictate we will all perish if we don't adhere to this offsetting of which "is" possible to achieve.

13. "Spiritual Transformation Of The Fourth Millennium" Old-time conventional religion is fading. New-time spirituality is on the rise. Objective realism is the prime issue here for future inclined thinking and believing.

14. "Understanding The Science Of Creative Mind" This is a study for discovering, developing and practicing a psychological powerhouse within for conquering the unconquerable, achieving the impossible or doing things no one has done all depending on, of course, the makeup and determination of the individual. This study brings out a greater potential of the individual's abilities when taken seriously. This was compiled from a lifetime of study and experience from your author.

15. "Living to 150" is a guidance program for intentions of anyone desiring a longer than longer life which is insightfully and innovatively educational for that purpose.

16. "The Act Of Getting One's Act Together" If anyone, business or nation wants to develop their stance, priorities and position in life, this is a chance for them to get their act together more than ever.

17. "Making Changes From This Point Forward" The design of this book is for the purpose of preventing repeated mistakes of unforeseen surprises due to what we weren't or aren't aware of that did, can or will happen again. It's all about gaining or rearranging change consciousness in this area.

18. "Relationships For All" This is a carefully arranged view of how relationships can function much better when initiated or guided by the experiences of many experts and your

author who have had failures and successes in their very human encounters. The experiences of more relationships result in wiser judgments and approaches to others.

19. "The We Between Us" helps us in discovering who is good for us and who is not. First it is a study in the book. Then it is a study with people of what exists in two party's minds (individuals business or nations) when first confronted. A real time saver in evaluating possible compatibility or not between the two for anyone. It works.

20. "Passion Of Dance" This is a narrative on progress, value and guidance for the dance inclined. It's informative and inspiring with its history and recent magnetism.

21. "Open That Door" to love. This book is comprehensively all about love. It's not a storybook. It clears up the differences of love

that causes misunderstanding, suspicion and deception.

22. "Get The Spirit" This book describes controversial and somewhat intertwined conventional views of spirit, spirits and spirituality. This book untangles the "usual" views and presents a more perspective manner of living with these concepts of mind.

23. "Stories Of What They Couldn't Or Wouldn't Tell" Ages are from babies to 100 years; twenty four of them.

24. "Improving On Love And Relationships" This one is two books in one. Part one "Open That Door" is a psychology of love that enhances perspective to understand and adapt to a very popular, but deceiving, repressed and ignored emotion; love. Part two covers "Relationships For All" which elaborates on origination, different types, significance, deceptions, desires, experiences,

communication, possibilities, future and guidance of relationships. It's comprehensive and also derived from a lifetime of relationship experiences and serious study.

NOTES

NOTES

NOTES

NOTES

NOTES